AF510274

AI and the Mind

AI and the Mind

Jeremiah Altman

First Printing, 2025

Contents

1

Introduction to AI and Cognition

The Intersection of AI and Human Mind

The intersection of AI and the human mind represents a burgeoning frontier that promises to enhance cognitive capabilities while carefully navigating the complexities of human cognition. As AI systems become more integrated into our daily lives, understanding how these tools can complement, rather than compromise, our mental faculties is essential. This synergy can lead to innovative applications that not only augment memory retention but also foster critical thinking and creativity, thus transforming the way we learn and interact with information.

AI tools designed for enhancing memory retention exemplify how technology can support cognitive processes. By leveraging algorithms that adapt to individual learning styles, these tools can provide personalized experiences that resonate with users. For instance, spaced repetition systems can optimize review schedules, ensuring that key information is reinforced at the most effective intervals. This approach not only improves recall but also reduces cognitive load, allowing learners to engage with complex material without feeling overwhelmed.

Cognitive load management is crucial in an age where information is abundant and distractions are prevalent. AI applications can play a significant role in streamlining information presentation and prioritizing tasks, thus enabling users to focus on what matters most. By employing intelligent filtering systems, individuals can minimize cognitive overload, allowing for better decision-making and enhanced productivity. This thoughtful integration of AI into our workflows can lead to a more efficient and focused approach to both personal and professional tasks.

Moreover, AI-powered learning platforms are emerging as vital tools in fostering critical thinking skills. These platforms can analyze user interactions and provide tailored feedback, encouraging learners to engage with material more deeply and thoughtfully. By promoting inquiry-based learning and problem-solving, these AI systems empower users to develop a robust cognitive toolkit that prepares them for real-world challenges. This shift towards a critical thinking framework exemplifies how AI can enrich our intellectual pursuits while still respecting the nuances of human thought.

As we navigate the ethical implications of AI's role in enhancing cognitive skills, mindfulness becomes a crucial aspect of this integration. Balancing automation with human creativity is essential, as over-reliance on AI may inadvertently stifle innovative thinking. By designing AI interfaces that prioritize mental clarity and encourage reflective practices, we can cultivate environments where technology and human intellect coexist harmoniously. This balanced approach not only respects the integrity of the human mind but also leverages AI's strengths to inspire new levels of cognitive development and creativity.

Overview of Cognitive Enhancement

Cognitive enhancement has emerged as a vital area of interest, especially in the context of artificial intelligence and its transformative potential. This subchapter offers an overview of cognitive enhancement, focusing on how AI can be harnessed to improve mental faculties without compromising cognitive integrity. The intersection of AI and cognition presents unique opportunities for individuals and organizations to amplify their mental capabilities while ensuring ethical considerations are met. By understanding the principles and methodologies of cognitive enhancement, AI enthusiasts can engage with these technologies in ways that genuinely augment human cognition.

One of the most promising applications of AI in cognitive enhancement is through tools designed to improve memory retention. AI-powered applications can analyze users' learning patterns and adapt content delivery to maximize retention. These tools may incorporate spaced repetition algorithms, tailored quizzes, and interactive content that aligns with individual cognitive profiles. By utilizing AI to personalize learning experiences, users can experience significant improvements in their memory, making it easier to recall information when needed, thereby enriching their educational and professional pursuits.

Cognitive load management is another critical aspect where AI can play a transformative role. AI applications can assist users in organizing information and prioritizing tasks, ultimately reducing cognitive overload. By intelligently filtering distractions and presenting only relevant data, AI tools can help maintain focus and clarity. This approach not only enhances productivity but also fosters a healthier cognitive environment where individuals can thrive without the constant pressure of competing information. Effective cognitive load management is essential in today's fast-paced world, where information saturation can hinder performance.

Mindfulness and AI integration provide an innovative pathway to better focus and mental well-being. AI can facilitate mindfulness practices through guided meditations, personalized reminders for breaks, and even real-time feedback on stress levels. By incorporating these tools into daily routines, individuals can cultivate a more focused mindset and enhance their overall cognitive performance. The synergy between mindfulness practices and AI technology can create an environment conducive to critical thinking and creativity, ensuring that users can maximize their cognitive potential without the detrimental effects of stress and distraction.

Ethical considerations remain paramount in the discourse surrounding cognitive enhancement through AI. It is crucial to balance automation and human creativity, ensuring that AI serves as a tool to augment rather than diminish human capabilities. By promoting ethical AI use, developers and users alike can foster environments where cognitive skills are enhanced responsibly. Furthermore, research into AI's impact on attention span and cognitive function can guide the development of tools that enhance rather than impair cognitive abilities. As we navigate this evolving landscape, it is vital for AI enthusiasts to advocate for personalized and ethical approaches to cognitive enhancement that respect and elevate human cognition.

2

Using AI Without Impairing Cognition

Understanding Cognitive Impairment Risks

Understanding cognitive impairment risks is essential for those involved in the intersection of artificial intelligence and cognitive enhancement. As AI tools become increasingly prevalent, it is crucial to recognize how these technologies may affect cognitive functions. While AI has the potential to enhance learning and memory retention, it can also pose risks if not designed and implemented thoughtfully. This subchapter explores the nuances of these risks and provides insights on how to mitigate them for the benefit of users.

Cognitive impairment can manifest in various forms, including reduced attention span, memory deficits, and difficulties in critical thinking. The integration of AI into daily tasks often leads to an increased cognitive load, as users navigate multiple platforms and tools that demand their attention. Understanding how AI impacts cognitive functions allows enthusiasts to tailor their approaches, ensuring that the benefits of AI do not come at the cost of mental clarity or cognitive health. By recognizing and addressing these risks, AI enthusiasts can create solutions that enhance rather than hinder cognitive processes.

One significant risk associated with AI tools is the potential for cognitive overload. When users are bombarded with information and options, it can lead to decision fatigue and diminished focus. AI applications that prioritize user experience should be designed to manage cognitive load effectively, allowing individuals to engage with information without becoming overwhelmed. By implementing features that streamline processes and reduce unnecessary distractions, developers can help users maintain their cognitive faculties while benefiting from AI advancements.

Moreover, ethical considerations play a vital role in the responsible use of AI for cognitive enhancement. The design of AI interfaces should promote mental clarity and support users in maintaining their cognitive skills. This includes fostering environments where creativity can flourish alongside automation, ensuring that AI serves as a tool for augmentation rather than a replacement for human ingenuity. By focusing on ethical principles, AI developers can create systems that enhance cognitive abilities while safeguarding against potential impairments.

Ultimately, the goal of understanding cognitive impairment risks is to harness the power of AI in a way that supports cognitive development and critical thinking. Personalized AI learning experiences can be developed to cater to individual cognitive needs, enabling users to engage with material in a manner that enhances retention and understanding. By prioritizing mindfulness and integrating AI thoughtfully, both developers and users can work together to create AI-powered learning environments that not only foster cognitive growth but also promote a sustainable balance between technology and human cognition.

Strategies for Responsible AI Use

The integration of artificial intelligence into our daily cognitive processes presents a significant opportunity for enhancing mental capabilities while maintaining ethical standards. To harness AI effectively, enthusiasts must prioritize transparency in AI algorithms. By understanding how these systems work, users can make informed decisions about their interaction with AI tools. This transparency fosters a culture of trust and encourages users to critically evaluate the information provided by AI, thereby preventing overreliance and promoting cognitive engagement.

Moreover, the design of AI interfaces should focus on minimizing cognitive overload. Intuitive design principles can help users to navigate AI tools efficiently, allowing for a seamless experience that enhances memory retention and reduces distractions. Features such as customizable dashboards, clear feedback mechanisms, and succinct information presentation can empower users to utilize AI for cognitive enhancement without overwhelming their mental faculties. By prioritizing user experience, we can create AI applications that enhance rather than detract from our cognitive capabilities.

In addition to interface design, the promotion of critical thinking should be a cornerstone of AI-powered learning platforms. These platforms can incorporate features that encourage users to question AI-generated content, engage in discussions, and explore alternative viewpoints. By fostering a mindset of inquiry, users are less likely to accept information at face value and more inclined to think critically about the material. This approach not only enhances cognitive skills but also prepares individuals to navigate an increasingly complex information landscape.

Mindfulness practices can be seamlessly integrated with AI technologies to improve focus and cognitive clarity. By employing AI tools that promote mindfulness, such as guided meditation applications or focus-enhancing environments, users can cultivate an awareness of their cognitive states.

This balance between technology and mindfulness can lead to improved attention spans and a reduction in cognitive biases, allowing for a more nuanced understanding of AI's role in cognitive development. Encouraging users to integrate mindful practices into their AI usage can ultimately enhance their overall cognitive health.

Lastly, a commitment to ethical AI use is essential in the pursuit of cognitive enhancement. Developers and users alike should consider the implications of AI on cognitive skills and strive for solutions that prioritize human creativity alongside automation. By establishing guidelines that promote responsible AI use, we can ensure that the technology serves to enrich our cognitive faculties rather than diminish them. This balanced approach will not only bolster individual cognitive development but also foster a healthy relationship between humans and AI.

3

AI Tools for Enhancing Memory Retention

Memory Techniques Enhanced by AI

Memory techniques have long been a subject of interest for cognitive scientists and educators alike, but the advent of artificial intelligence offers an unprecedented opportunity to enhance these methods. By leveraging AI, individuals can access personalized memory aids that cater to their unique cognitive profiles. This customization allows learners to utilize techniques such as spaced repetition, mnemonics, and visual imagery in a way that resonates with their personal learning styles, thus improving retention and recall. AI algorithms can analyze user interactions and suggest optimal learning strategies, making the process both efficient and effective.

AI-powered learning platforms are at the forefront of this transformation. These platforms employ adaptive learning technologies that adjust content delivery based on a user's performance and engagement levels. For instance, by using data analytics, these systems can determine which memory techniques yield the best results for a specific learner, providing targeted exercises that reinforce memory retention. This personalized approach not only enhances cognitive capabilities but also fosters critical thinking by encouraging users to engage with material at deeper levels, rather than merely memorizing facts.

Cognitive load management is another crucial aspect where AI can play a significant role. By automating repetitive and mundane tasks, AI tools free up cognitive resources, allowing individuals to focus on more complex problem-solving activities. This balance between automation and human creativity is essential in workplaces, where cognitive overload can stifle innovation. AI can streamline workflows, ensuring that mental energy is directed toward tasks that require critical thinking and creativity, ultimately enhancing overall productivity.

The integration of mindfulness practices with AI technology can further improve focus and memory. AI applications that promote mindfulness encourage users to take regular breaks, practice meditation, or engage in reflective exercises, thereby reducing stress and enhancing cognitive function. By creating a harmonious relationship between human cognition and AI support, individuals can achieve better mental clarity, which is vital for effective memory retention. This synergy not only benefits personal learning but also contributes to healthier work environments.

Ethical considerations in the use of AI for cognitive enhancement cannot be overlooked. As we explore AI strategies for reducing cognitive bias and fostering personalized learning experiences, it is essential to ensure that these tools are designed with a focus on promoting human well-being. By prioritizing transparency and user control, developers can create AI systems that empower users rather than diminish their cognitive abilities. As research continues to emerge regarding AI's impact on attention span and cognitive function, a careful approach will ensure that these technologies serve as allies in the quest for enhanced cognition without compromise.

Case Studies of Successful AI Applications

Case studies of successful AI applications provide a rich tapestry of insights into how artificial intelligence can enhance human cognition without compromising it. One notable example is the implementation of AI-driven learning platforms in educational institutions, which have revolutionized how students interact with information. These platforms utilize adaptive learning technologies to assess individual learning styles and paces, tailoring content to maximize engagement and retention. By continuously analyzing student performance, they reduce cognitive load, allowing learners to focus on critical thinking rather than rote memorization. This personalized approach not only fosters deeper understanding but also encourages autonomy in the learning process.

Another compelling case is the use of AI in mental health applications aimed at improving mindfulness and focus. Platforms like Woebot employ conversational AI to provide users with cognitive behavioral therapy techniques in a readily accessible format. Through regular interactions, users can develop greater self-awareness and mindfulness practices, which have been shown to enhance attention span and mental clarity. These applications exemplify how AI can serve as a supportive tool, guiding users through their mental health journeys while promoting skills that lead to improved cognitive performance.

In the workplace, AI tools designed for balancing automation and human creativity have emerged as vital assets. Companies like Adobe have integrated AI to assist creatives in generating content while allowing them to maintain control over the creative process. These tools help streamline repetitive tasks, thereby reducing cognitive load and freeing up mental resources for more innovative thinking. By fostering an environment where

AI complements human creativity rather than replacing it, organizations can drive productivity while enhancing employees' cognitive skills and job satisfaction.

Ethical considerations are paramount in the development of AI applications intended to enhance cognitive skills. Research has shown that AI can inadvertently reinforce cognitive biases, which can lead to skewed decision-making processes. Companies focused on ethical AI use are implementing strategies to mitigate these biases, such as training models on diverse datasets and incorporating feedback loops that allow for continuous learning and improvement. By prioritizing ethical applications, these organizations not only advance technology but also contribute to a more informed and fair decision-making landscape, which is crucial for cognitive development.

Finally, research on AI's impact on attention span and cognitive function has led to innovative strategies for reducing distractions in learning environments. One such strategy involves the design of AI interfaces that promote mental clarity by minimizing unnecessary stimuli. By leveraging user-centered design principles, these interfaces help users maintain focus on their tasks, ultimately enhancing cognitive performance. As AI continues to evolve, the lessons learned from these case studies will inform future developments, ensuring that technology serves as a catalyst for cognitive enhancement rather than a hindrance.

4

Cognitive Load Management in AI Applications

Defining Cognitive Load

Cognitive load refers to the total amount of mental effort being used in the working memory. This concept is essential for understanding how individuals process and retain information, especially in an age where artificial intelligence tools are becoming increasingly prevalent. Cognitive load can be divided into three types: intrinsic, extraneous, and germane. Intrinsic load relates to the inherent difficulty of the material itself, extraneous load involves how the information is presented, and germane load refers to the mental effort dedicated to processing and understanding the material. For AI enthusiasts, grasping these distinctions is vital as it lays the groundwork for optimizing technology that complements human cognition.

In the context of AI applications, managing cognitive load is crucial for enhancing user experience and effectiveness. AI tools can either alleviate or exacerbate cognitive load, depending on their design and implementation. For instance, an AI-powered learning platform that presents information in a clear, engaging manner can reduce extraneous load, allowing users to focus more on understanding and retaining knowledge. Conversely, poorly designed interfaces or overwhelming amounts of information can increase cognitive load, leading to frustration and diminished learning outcomes. Therefore, understanding cognitive load is essential for developing AI solutions that genuinely enhance cognitive capabilities without overwhelming users.

AI's potential to enhance memory retention is particularly noteworthy, as it can personalize learning experiences tailored to individual cognitive profiles. By leveraging data analytics, AI can identify a user's strengths and weaknesses, adjusting the difficulty and presentation of information accordingly. This personalized approach not only fosters better retention but also encourages a deeper engagement with the material. When cognitive load is managed effectively, learners are more likely to achieve a state of flow, where they can immerse themselves in their learning without the distraction of cognitive overload.

Furthermore, the intersection of mindfulness and AI integration presents an innovative frontier for promoting better focus and cognitive clarity. Mindfulness practices can help individuals become aware of their cognitive load, allowing them to manage their mental resources more effectively. AI can support this by providing tools that encourage mindful interaction with technology, such as reminders to take breaks or prompts for reflection. By creating an environment where users can cultivate focus, AI can enhance cognitive function while also respecting the need for human creativity and intuition.

As we navigate the future of AI in cognitive development, ethical considerations must be at the forefront of our discussions. The goal should not be to replace human cognitive skills but to augment them in a way that is responsible and respectful. Strategies to reduce cognitive bias through AI can empower users to make more informed decisions, while also fostering critical thinking skills. By ensuring that AI systems are designed with cognitive load in mind, we can create a balanced relationship between automation and human creativity, ultimately leading to a more effective and thoughtful integration of AI in our daily lives.

AI Solutions for Reducing Cognitive Overload

In the quest to improve cognitive efficiency, AI solutions have emerged as powerful allies in reducing cognitive overload. This phenomenon, characterized by an overwhelming amount of information and tasks that can lead to mental fatigue, has become increasingly relevant in our fast-paced digital world. By leveraging AI technologies, we can create systems that intelligently filter information, prioritize tasks, and provide personalized insights tailored to individual cognitive capacities. This not only alleviates the burden on our mental faculties but also enhances our ability to process and retain information effectively.

AI tools designed to enhance memory retention play a significant role in combating cognitive overload. These applications utilize algorithms that adapt to users' learning styles, helping to reinforce knowledge through spaced repetition and active recall techniques. By integrating these methods into daily learning routines, individuals can experience improved retention rates without the stress of cramming information. Furthermore, such tools can seamlessly blend with existing educational frameworks, offering a supportive environment that encourages deeper understanding and long-term knowledge retention.

Cognitive load management is another critical area where AI can make a profound impact. Through data analysis and user feedback, AI systems can identify when users are reaching their cognitive limits and adjust the flow of information accordingly. This dynamic approach not only prevents overwhelm but also fosters an environment where critical thinking can thrive. By providing prompts and suggestions that align with the user's current cognitive state, AI applications can cultivate a more engaged and focused learning experience, thereby enhancing overall cognitive performance.

The design of AI interfaces also significantly influences mental clarity. Intuitive and user-friendly interfaces can reduce extraneous cognitive load, allowing users to concentrate on essential tasks. By employing principles of cognitive psychology in interface design, developers can create tools that facilitate efficient interaction without adding unnecessary complexity. This thoughtful approach ensures that users can engage with technology in a way that complements their cognitive processes rather than hinders them, promoting a balanced relationship between human creativity and automation.

Lastly, the ethical use of AI in enhancing cognitive skills must not be overlooked. As we embrace AI solutions, it is crucial to maintain a focus on user autonomy and the preservation of critical thinking abilities. By designing AI systems that encourage mindful interaction and foster a sense of agency, we can create environments where cognitive skills are not just enhanced but also respected. This holistic approach ensures that AI serves as a tool for empowerment rather than a crutch, allowing individuals to navigate the complexities of information with clarity and confidence.

5

AI-Powered Learning Platforms that Foster Critical

Features of Effective Learning Platforms

Effective learning platforms harness the power of artificial intelligence to create environments that not only enhance cognitive abilities but also respect the natural learning processes of the mind. At the core of these platforms is personalization, which tailors educational experiences to the individual learner's needs, preferences, and pace. This adaptability ensures that users engage with content that resonates with their existing knowledge and learning styles, facilitating deeper understanding and retention. By analyzing user interactions and feedback, AI can modify the learning path dynamically, allowing learners to explore concepts thoroughly without overwhelming them.

Another essential feature of effective learning platforms is their capacity for cognitive load management. By breaking down complex information into digestible segments and employing techniques such as spaced repetition and interleaved practice, these platforms help learners manage their cognitive resources efficiently. This approach prevents cognitive overload, ensuring that learners can absorb and retain information without feeling stressed. Incorporating visual aids, interactive elements, and gamified experiences can further enhance engagement, allowing users to focus on learning rather than struggling with excessive information.

Critical thinking is a crucial skill in today's information-rich world, and effective learning platforms integrate AI tools that promote this competency. By presenting learners with real-world problems and encouraging them to analyze, evaluate, and create solutions, these platforms foster an environment where critical thinking thrives. AI can simulate various scenarios, challenge assumptions, and provide immediate feedback, prompting learners to refine their thought processes. This not only enhances cognitive skills but also prepares learners to navigate complex issues in practical settings.

Mindfulness is increasingly recognized as a vital component of effective learning, and AI-powered platforms can incorporate mindfulness practices to boost focus and clarity. Features such as guided meditation sessions, focus timers, and reminders for breaks can help learners cultivate a balanced mental state conducive to learning. By integrating these techniques, platforms encourage users to be present and engaged, which is essential for effective retention and application of knowledge. This holistic approach to learning helps to maintain mental clarity amidst the distractions of modern life.

Lastly, ethical considerations play a significant role in the design of AI-powered learning platforms. Developers must prioritize transparency and user well-being, ensuring that AI tools enhance cognitive skills without compromising mental health. This involves creating interfaces that are intuitive and user-friendly, minimizing distractions while promoting deep engagement. Furthermore, addressing cognitive biases through AI strategies fosters a more equitable learning environment, enabling learners to approach information critically and develop their skills in a fair setting. Balancing automation with human creativity is essential to create a sustainable, effective learning ecosystem that empowers learners without impairing their cognitive functions.

Examples of AI-driven Critical Thinking Tools

AI-driven critical thinking tools have emerged as transformative assets in the quest to enhance human cognition while maintaining mental clarity. These tools leverage advanced algorithms and data analytics to foster analytical reasoning and promote deeper understanding across various domains. One prominent example is AI-powered tutoring systems that adapt to individual learning styles. By analyzing a learner's performance in real-time, these systems can provide personalized feedback and resources, effectively guiding users through complex problem-solving scenarios. This tailored approach not only aids memory retention but also cultivates critical thinking skills by challenging users to engage with material in a meaningful way.

Another noteworthy example is the integration of AI in collaborative platforms, which facilitate brainstorming and idea generation. Tools like MindMeister and Miro utilize AI to suggest connections between concepts, allowing teams to explore multiple perspectives before arriving at a conclusion. This functionality helps to reduce cognitive load by organizing thoughts visually and encouraging a structured approach to problem-solving. By supporting collaborative efforts, these platforms enhance cognitive flexibility and promote a culture of creativity within workplaces, making them invaluable for teams striving to balance automation and human ingenuity.

AI-driven research tools also play a crucial role in critical thinking enhancement. Platforms like Semantic Scholar use machine learning to sift through vast amounts of academic literature, identifying relevant studies and summarizing key findings. This capability not only saves time but also enriches users' understanding by exposing them to diverse viewpoints and methodologies. Such tools empower researchers and students to engage critically with existing knowledge, enabling them to formulate well-informed arguments and hypotheses. By streamlining the research process, these AI solutions promote a more thorough consideration of evidence, fostering a culture of intellectual rigor.

Mindfulness applications that incorporate AI offer another innovative approach to enhancing cognitive function. Tools such as Headspace and Calm use artificial intelligence to personalize meditation and mindfulness practices, helping users cultivate focus and reduce stress. By encouraging users to engage in reflective thinking, these applications support mental clarity and resilience. Through guided sessions that adapt to individual needs, these tools reinforce the importance of mindfulness in maintaining cognitive health, ultimately allowing users to approach challenges with heightened awareness and creativity.

Lastly, AI strategies aimed at reducing cognitive bias are critical for fostering better decision-making. Tools like Cognitune leverage machine learning to analyze patterns in decision-making processes, identifying common biases that may influence outcomes. By making users aware of these biases and offering alternative perspectives, these tools promote a more balanced approach to thinking and problem-solving. This awareness is essential in a world where information overload can cloud judgment, and integrating such AI-driven insights into daily practices can significantly enhance cognitive capabilities. Through these diverse applications, AI is proving to be a powerful ally in the pursuit of critical thinking and cognitive development.

6

Mindfulness and AI Integration for Better Focus

The Role of Mindfulness in Cognitive Function

The integration of mindfulness into cognitive function is a compelling area of exploration, particularly for AI enthusiasts keen on enhancing human cognition without compromising mental clarity. Mindfulness, defined as the practice of maintaining a moment-by-moment awareness of our thoughts, feelings, bodily sensations, and surrounding environment, holds significant potential for improving cognitive processes. By cultivating mindfulness, individuals can enhance their focus, reduce cognitive load, and improve their memory retention, all essential components for effective interaction with AI tools. As we delve deeper into the interplay between mindfulness and cognitive function, it becomes evident that these practices can complement the technological advancements we pursue in AI.

One of the primary benefits of mindfulness is its ability to enhance attention span. In a world increasingly influenced by AI, where distractions are ubiquitous, maintaining focus can be challenging. Mindfulness practices train the brain to resist distractions, allowing individuals to engage more fully with AI applications designed for learning and productivity. This heightened focus not only bolsters cognitive function but also ensures that users can leverage AI tools more effectively, leading to improved outcomes in tasks that require sustained attention. By reducing cognitive overload, mindfulness enables individuals to navigate complex AI interfaces with greater ease and mental clarity.

Moreover, the impact of mindfulness on memory retention is particularly relevant for those utilizing AI-powered learning platforms. Research indicates that mindfulness can enhance working memory, which is crucial for processing and retaining information. As learners interact with AI systems that personalize educational experiences, incorporating mindfulness techniques can further amplify these benefits. By fostering an environment where learners are mentally present and engaged, we can optimize the learning potential of AI technologies. This symbiotic relationship not only supports cognitive development but also encourages critical thinking skills essential for navigating an AI-driven future.

Cognitive load management is another vital aspect where mindfulness can play a transformative role. As AI applications become more sophisticated, they often present users with overwhelming amounts of information. Mindfulness practices can help individuals manage this cognitive load by promoting a more balanced approach to information processing. By encouraging users to break tasks into smaller, more manageable components and to remain present in the moment, mindfulness can enhance decision-making and problem-solving abilities. This approach aligns seamlessly with the goal of designing AI interfaces that are intuitive and supportive of mental clarity.

Finally, the ethical implications of integrating mindfulness with AI cannot be overlooked. As we strive to enhance cognitive skills through AI, it is imperative to consider the potential biases that may arise in automated systems. Mindfulness encourages self-awareness and reflection, equipping users with the tools to recognize and address cognitive biases that may influence their interactions with AI. This awareness fosters a more equitable use of technology, ensuring that AI advancements serve to enhance human creativity rather than diminish it. By prioritizing mindfulness within the framework of AI development, we can create a future where technology and human cognition coexist harmoniously, driving innovation while preserving the integrity of the mind.

AI Tools that Support Mindfulness Practices

AI tools have emerged as valuable allies in fostering mindfulness practices, offering innovative approaches to enhance cognitive well-being without compromising mental clarity. These tools leverage advanced algorithms and data analytics to create personalized experiences that help individuals cultivate awareness and presence in their daily lives. By integrating AI into mindfulness practices, users can benefit from tailored guidance, progress tracking, and interactive features that encourage deeper engagement.

One significant area where AI tools excel is in providing customized mindfulness routines. Through the use of machine learning, these applications can analyze user behavior and preferences to suggest personalized meditation sessions, breathing exercises, or mindfulness activities. This level of customization not only enhances user experience but also promotes greater adherence to mindfulness practices, thereby improving overall cognitive function and emotional regulation. As a result, individuals are more likely to develop sustainable habits that support their mental health.

AI-powered platforms also facilitate cognitive load management by offering users the ability to schedule mindfulness breaks effectively. By employing intelligent algorithms, these tools can assess users' workloads and stress levels, prompting them to take necessary pauses. This integration of mindfulness into daily routines helps mitigate the effects of cognitive overload, allowing users to recharge and refocus. Such strategic interventions are crucial in maintaining optimal cognitive performance, especially in high-demand environments where attention and mental clarity are paramount.

Moreover, the use of AI in mindfulness practices can foster critical thinking by encouraging users to reflect on their thoughts and emotions. Many AI-driven mindfulness applications incorporate journaling features that allow users to document their experiences and insights. These reflective practices not only enhance self-awareness but also promote cognitive development by challenging users to analyze their thought patterns and biases. In this way, AI tools serve as a bridge between mindfulness and cognitive growth, facilitating a deeper understanding of oneself and the world.

Finally, ethical considerations surrounding AI usage in mindfulness practices cannot be overlooked. As these tools become more integrated into daily life, it is essential to ensure that they are designed with user well-being in mind. Developers must prioritize transparency, privacy, and user consent, ensuring that individuals feel safe and empowered while using AI for mindfulness. By balancing automation with human creativity and ethical practices, AI can significantly enhance cognitive skills and promote a mindful approach to technological integration in our lives.

7

Designing AI Interfaces Promoting Mental Clarity

Principles of User-Centric Design

User-centric design is a foundational principle that emphasizes the importance of tailoring technology to the needs, preferences, and limitations of users. In the context of AI applications, this principle becomes even more critical as we strive to enhance cognitive abilities without compromising mental clarity or well-being. By placing users at the center of the design process, developers can create AI tools that not only support memory retention but also manage cognitive load effectively. This approach encourages the development of interfaces that are intuitive, allowing users to engage with AI in a way that complements their natural thought processes.

To implement user-centric design in AI, it is essential to conduct thorough user research. Understanding the specific needs of different user demographics enables designers to create personalized experiences that address individual cognitive strengths and weaknesses. For instance, an AI-powered learning platform designed for students might incorporate elements that foster critical thinking and adaptability, while tools aimed at professionals may focus on enhancing productivity through efficient task management. By gathering insights directly from users, designers can ensure that their solutions are relevant and effective, ultimately leading to improved cognitive outcomes.

Another vital aspect of user-centric design is the emphasis on accessibility. AI tools must be designed to accommodate a wide range of cognitive abilities and learning styles. This includes providing customizable interfaces that allow users to adjust settings according to their preferences, which can help in reducing cognitive bias and enhancing focus. By incorporating features like adjustable text sizes, color contrast, and varied content formats, developers can create inclusive environments that promote mental clarity and allow all users to thrive.

Moreover, ethical considerations play a significant role in user-centric design. As AI systems have the potential to influence cognitive skills and decision-making processes, it is crucial to ensure that these technologies are used responsibly. Designers must be mindful of how AI applications can inadvertently reinforce cognitive biases or overwhelm users with information. By prioritizing transparency and ethical guidelines in the design process, developers can build trust and facilitate a healthy relationship between users and AI, ultimately enhancing cognitive development without compromising mental wellness.

Finally, the iterative nature of user-centric design allows for continuous improvement based on user feedback. Engaging users in the testing and refinement stages ensures that AI applications evolve in alignment with their needs. This ongoing dialogue fosters a culture of mindfulness, where users feel empowered to share their experiences and contribute to the creation of tools that genuinely enhance their cognitive abilities. By embracing a user-centric approach, AI enthusiasts can drive innovation that not only advances technology but also supports the mental faculties of individuals, paving the way for a future where AI and human cognition harmoniously coexist.

Best Practices for AI Interface Development

In the rapidly evolving landscape of AI, developing interfaces that prioritize user cognition is paramount. Best practices for AI interface development begin with a deep understanding of human cognitive processes. Designers must consider how users interact with technology and ensure that the interface is intuitive and supportive. This means leveraging principles from cognitive psychology to create environments that minimize cognitive load, allowing users to engage with AI tools without feeling overwhelmed. A well-designed interface can facilitate smoother interactions, ensuring that users can focus on enhancing their cognitive skills rather than struggling with complicated navigation.

Another essential aspect is the integration of mindfulness principles within AI interfaces. By incorporating features that promote mindfulness, such as reminders for breaks or prompts for reflection, developers can foster an environment conducive to mental clarity. These features should be seamlessly integrated into the user experience, allowing users to engage in critical thinking and reflection without disrupting their workflow. Furthermore, interfaces should be designed to encourage focused engagement, reducing distractions that can lead to cognitive overload and impair memory retention.

In addition to mindfulness, ethical considerations must guide the development of AI interfaces. Designers should prioritize transparency in AI functionality, allowing users to understand how their data is being used and how AI recommendations are generated. This transparency builds trust and encourages users to engage more deeply with AI tools, enhancing cognitive development. Ethical design also involves considering the potential for cognitive bias in AI algorithms and ensuring that these tools do not reinforce existing biases, which is critical for fostering critical thinking and promoting equitable cognitive enhancement.

Personalization is another best practice that can significantly enhance the effectiveness of AI interfaces. By tailoring experiences to individual user needs, preferences, and learning styles, developers can create environments that facilitate better cognitive engagement. Personalized AI learning experiences can adapt to the user's pace and provide targeted support, promoting deeper understanding and retention of information. This adaptability ensures that users are not subjected to a one-size-fits-all approach, which can often lead to frustration and disengagement.

Finally, balancing automation and human creativity is crucial in AI interface development. While AI can handle repetitive tasks and analyze vast amounts of data, it is essential that users retain the ability to express creativity and critical thinking. Interfaces should encourage users to explore ideas and innovate, rather than simply relying on automated suggestions. By fostering a collaborative relationship between humans and AI, developers can create tools that enhance cognitive skills while preserving the unique qualities of human thought. This balance is vital in cultivating a future where AI serves as an empowering ally in cognitive development rather than a hindrance.

8

Balancing Automation and Human Creativity

Understanding Automation's Role in Creativity

Automation's role in creativity is a nuanced subject that warrants careful exploration. As AI enthusiasts, it is vital to recognize that, while automation can streamline tasks and enhance productivity, it should not be seen merely as a replacement for human creativity. Instead, automation can serve as a powerful tool that complements and amplifies creative processes, allowing individuals to focus on higher-level thinking and innovation. By leveraging AI technologies, creators can spend less time on mundane tasks and more time on ideation and experimentation, thus fostering an environment where creativity can flourish.

In the realm of cognitive load management, automation can significantly alleviate the mental burden associated with routine tasks. For instance, AI-powered tools can handle data organization, scheduling, and even preliminary research, freeing up cognitive resources for more complex problem-solving and creative endeavors. This shift in focus enables individuals to engage in deeper cognitive processes, which are essential for innovation. By reducing the cognitive load, AI allows for a more profound exploration of ideas, encouraging creative breakthroughs that might not have been possible under traditional workflows.

Moreover, AI tools designed for enhancing memory retention can play a crucial role in the creative process. These tools can help individuals organize their thoughts, track ideas, and even suggest connections between seemingly unrelated concepts. Such functionality not only aids in maintaining a clear cognitive pathway but also stimulates creative thinking by providing a broader context for ideas. As learners interact with these platforms, they can develop a richer understanding of their own creative processes, leading to more effective and innovative outcomes.

The integration of mindfulness practices with AI also holds promise for enhancing focus and creativity. Mindful use of AI can create a balanced environment where technology serves as a facilitator rather than a distraction. By designing AI interfaces that promote mental clarity and reduce cognitive overload, users can engage more fully in their creative tasks. This harmonious relationship between mindfulness and AI ensures that automation enhances cognitive skills without compromising the unique human elements of creativity, such as intuition and emotional insight.

Lastly, ethical considerations in the use of AI for enhancing cognitive skills cannot be overlooked. It is essential to strike a balance between leveraging automation and maintaining the integrity of human creativity. Responsible AI deployment must prioritize transparency, fairness, and inclusivity, ensuring that these systems enhance rather than hinder creative expression. By adopting ethical practices, we can cultivate an innovative landscape where automation serves as a complementary force to human creativity, ultimately leading to richer, more diverse outcomes in artistic and intellectual pursuits.

Strategies for Enhancing Human-AI Collaboration

Strategies for enhancing human-AI collaboration can be pivotal in ensuring that AI technologies serve as true partners in cognitive tasks rather than mere tools. One of the foremost strategies involves the design of AI systems that complement human cognitive strengths while mitigating weaknesses. For instance, AI can be utilized to handle data processing and analysis, allowing individuals to focus on higher-level cognitive tasks such as critical thinking and creativity. This division of labor not only enhances productivity but also encourages users to engage more deeply with their work, fostering an environment where human insight and machine efficiency coalesce.

Another effective strategy is the integration of AI tools that promote memory retention and cognitive load management. By leveraging AI's capability to tailor content delivery based on individual learning styles and paces, users can experience personalized learning journeys that bolster their memory retention. These AI-powered platforms can also employ techniques such as spaced repetition, helping to reduce the cognitive load during learning sessions. This targeted approach ensures that users are not overwhelmed, allowing them to absorb information more effectively and apply it in practical scenarios.

Furthermore, fostering critical thinking through AI-powered learning platforms is essential for enhancing cognitive collaboration. AI can facilitate discussions, pose challenging questions, and provide diverse perspectives that stimulate critical analysis. By creating interactive learning environments where learners can engage with AI as both a source of information and a collaborative partner, individuals can develop their analytical skills in a supportive framework. This strategy not only enriches the learning experience but also prepares users to navigate complex problems in real-world contexts.

Mindfulness integration with AI technologies can also significantly improve focus and mental clarity. By designing AI interfaces that encourage mindful interactions, users can cultivate a more intentional approach to their tasks. Tools that prompt users to take breaks, reflect on their work, or practice mindfulness exercises can help maintain mental clarity and enhance overall cognitive function. This mindful approach ensures that users remain engaged and present in their tasks, ultimately leading to improved productivity and satisfaction.

Lastly, addressing ethical considerations in AI use is paramount for fostering a balanced relationship between human creativity and machine assistance. Strategies that focus on transparency, accountability, and the reduction of cognitive biases in AI algorithms can empower users to make informed decisions. By ensuring that AI systems are designed to promote fairness and inclusivity, we can cultivate an environment where human creativity thrives alongside automation. This balance is crucial not only for enhancing cognitive skills but also for establishing a sustainable and ethical framework for future human-AI collaboration.

9

Ethical AI Use in Enhancing Cognitive Skills

Ethical Considerations in AI Development

Ethical considerations in AI development are paramount, especially in the context of enhancing human cognition without compromising individual autonomy or mental well-being. As AI enthusiasts, it is essential to recognize that the integration of artificial intelligence into cognitive enhancement tools must prioritize ethical frameworks that safeguard user autonomy and promote mental clarity. This involves a commitment to transparency in AI algorithms, ensuring that users understand how their data is utilized and how decisions are made. By fostering an environment of trust, developers can enhance the efficacy of AI tools while empowering users to engage critically with technology.

The impact of AI on memory retention and cognitive load management necessitates careful ethical scrutiny. AI applications that aim to enhance memory should be designed to complement human cognition rather than replace or diminish it. This raises questions about the potential overreliance on technology, which could inadvertently lead to cognitive atrophy. An ethical approach requires developers to encourage balanced usage, providing guidance and resources that promote mindful engagement with AI tools. Striking this balance will ensure that users benefit from enhanced memory retention while maintaining their cognitive skills.

AI-powered learning platforms present an opportunity to foster critical thinking and creativity while adhering to ethical standards. These platforms can be designed to challenge users, encouraging them to question information and engage in reflective thinking rather than passively consuming content. Developers should prioritize features that promote active learning and discourage cognitive shortcuts, which can lead to biases and superficial understanding. By creating learning experiences that stimulate curiosity and critical analysis, AI can serve as a catalyst for cognitive growth rather than a hindrance.

The intersection of mindfulness and AI integration is another area ripe for ethical exploration. Mindfulness applications powered by AI can help users focus and manage their cognitive load effectively. However, it is crucial to ensure that these tools do not exploit users' vulnerabilities or promote unhealthy patterns of dependence. Ethical AI development in this realm should prioritize user well-being, creating features that encourage users to take breaks, reflect, and engage in self-care. By fostering an ethical framework that promotes mental health, developers can create a healthier relationship between users and technology.

Finally, as we consider the balance between automation and human creativity in workplaces, ethical considerations become even more critical. AI tools designed to enhance cognitive skills should augment human creativity rather than replace it. Developers must ensure that their AI interfaces promote collaboration and support innovative thinking. This involves creating systems that respect human input and creativity, allowing users to retain agency in their work processes. By prioritizing ethical AI use, we can harness the potential of artificial intelligence to enhance cognitive development while preserving the essence of human creativity and critical thought.

Guidelines for Ethical AI Practices

In the journey of integrating artificial intelligence into cognitive enhancement, it is essential to establish a framework of ethical practices that prioritize the well-being and cognitive integrity of users. The first guideline emphasizes transparency in AI systems. Developers and organizations should clearly communicate the functionalities and limitations of their AI tools. Users benefit from understanding how these systems operate, which fosters trust and enables informed decision-making. By being transparent, developers can demystify AI processes, allowing users to engage productively without fear of manipulation or misinformation.

Another crucial guideline is to prioritize user autonomy. AI should serve as a supportive tool that empowers individuals rather than controlling their actions or decisions. This means designing interfaces that encourage critical thinking and mindfulness, allowing users to maintain agency over their cognitive processes. In AI-powered learning platforms, for instance, incorporating features that promote self-directed learning can help users navigate their educational journey without becoming overly reliant on automated suggestions. This balance fosters resilience and adaptability in cognitive skills.

Additionally, it is vital to address cognitive load management in AI applications. Systems should be designed to minimize unnecessary cognitive strain, ensuring that users can focus on enhancing their cognitive abilities rather than feeling overwhelmed by information. This involves creating intuitive user experiences that facilitate easy navigation and comprehension. By streamlining interactions and presenting information in digestible formats, developers can help users maintain mental clarity and focus, ultimately improving their learning and retention outcomes.

Ethical AI practices must also consider the reduction of cognitive bias. AI developers should strive to create algorithms that recognize and mitigate biases inherent in data sets. By actively working to eliminate these biases, AI tools can provide more accurate and equitable outcomes, enhancing cognitive development across diverse user groups. Furthermore, promoting diverse datasets in training AI systems can ensure that a wide range of perspectives is considered, leading to fairer and more balanced AI applications.

Finally, fostering a collaborative environment between AI and human creativity is essential. Encouraging the use of AI as a partner in the creative process can enhance cognitive skills without undermining original thought. This approach not only amplifies human creativity but also allows individuals to leverage AI's strengths while maintaining their unique perspectives. By designing AI systems that complement human capabilities, we can create an ecosystem that nurtures cognitive growth and innovation, paving the way for a future where AI and human intellect coexist harmoniously.

10

AI Strategies for Reducing Cognitive Bias

Understanding Cognitive Bias

Cognitive bias refers to the systematic patterns of deviation from norm or rationality in judgment, leading individuals to make illogical conclusions or decisions. Understanding these biases is crucial for AI enthusiasts who seek to enhance cognitive functions without compromising mental clarity. By recognizing how cognitive biases shape our perceptions and decision-making processes, we can design AI tools that aid in mitigating these biases rather than exacerbating them. This understanding sets the foundation for creating AI applications that support critical thinking and promote better cognitive outcomes.

One of the most significant aspects of cognitive bias is its impact on memory retention. For instance, confirmation bias can lead individuals to favor information that aligns with their existing beliefs while dismissing contradictory evidence. In crafting AI tools that enhance memory retention, it is essential to consider how these biases can influence the information presented to users. By integrating features that encourage diverse viewpoints and challenge existing assumptions, AI can serve not only as a memory aid but also as a catalyst for broader cognitive engagement.

Cognitive load management is another critical area where understanding cognitive bias plays a vital role. Excessive cognitive load can hinder our ability to process information effectively, often leading to reliance on shortcuts driven by biases. AI applications designed with an awareness of cognitive biases can help streamline information delivery, reduce unnecessary cognitive load, and enhance user experience. For instance, adaptive learning platforms can adjust content complexity based on a learner's progress, ensuring that users are neither overwhelmed nor under-challenged, thus promoting optimal cognitive functioning.

The integration of mindfulness practices with AI also offers a unique opportunity to address cognitive bias. Mindfulness encourages awareness of one's thoughts and feelings, which can help individuals recognize their biases in real time. AI-powered tools can support this integration by providing reminders or prompts that encourage users to engage in mindfulness practices, fostering greater focus and mental clarity. By combining mindfulness techniques with AI, we can create environments that not only enhance cognitive skills but also promote ethical use of technology in cognitive development.

Lastly, personalized AI learning experiences can be tailored to counteract cognitive biases by adapting to individual learning styles and preferences. For example, AI systems can analyze user behavior to identify specific biases and adjust the learning content accordingly, promoting a more balanced perspective. This not only aids in cognitive development but also empowers users to become more aware of their thought processes. Research into AI's impact on attention span and cognitive function underscores the importance of designing interfaces that are intuitive and supportive, ensuring that automation complements rather than detracts from human creativity and critical thinking.

AI Interventions for Bias Reduction

Bias in decision-making can significantly impair cognitive processes, leading to skewed judgments and ineffective outcomes. As AI enthusiasts, it is essential to explore how artificial intelligence can serve as a powerful tool in reducing these biases. By leveraging machine learning algorithms and data analysis, AI can identify patterns in decision-making that may be influenced by cognitive biases, providing insights that can lead to more objective outcomes. These interventions can be integrated into various applications, from hiring processes to educational settings, fostering an environment where critical thinking is prioritized, and individual cognitive capacities are enhanced.

One notable approach is the implementation of AI systems that utilize diverse datasets to train algorithms, ensuring a broad range of perspectives is considered. This strategy helps in minimizing the risk of bias that often arises from homogeneous training data. For instance, in recruitment AI, incorporating a wide array of demographic information can help identify and mitigate biases that may favor certain groups over others. Consequently, this creates a more equitable selection process, allowing organizations to tap into diverse talents and perspectives, ultimately enhancing collective cognitive capabilities.

Furthermore, AI can assist in cognitive load management by streamlining information delivery and presenting data in ways that encourage critical thinking. By analyzing user interactions, AI systems can adapt content delivery to suit individual learning styles, thereby reducing cognitive overload. This personalized approach not only aids in memory retention but also fosters an environment conducive to deeper cognitive engagement. As users interact with these AI-powered platforms, they can develop critical thinking skills, enhancing their overall cognitive function without succumbing to the pitfalls of inherent biases.

Mindfulness and AI integration can also play a significant role in bias reduction. AI systems designed to promote mindfulness can help users focus on the present moment, reducing impulsive decision-making driven by cognitive biases. By employing techniques such as guided meditations or reflective prompts, these AI applications encourage users to evaluate their thought processes critically. This reflective practice can lead to more deliberate decision-making, allowing individuals to become more aware of their biases and how they may influence their judgments.

Finally, the ethical deployment of AI in bias reduction is paramount. As we develop AI systems aimed at enhancing cognitive skills, we must ensure that these technologies do not inadvertently reinforce existing biases. A commitment to transparency and accountability in AI design will help in creating tools that empower users to recognize and confront their cognitive biases. By fostering a culture of ethical AI use, we can cultivate environments where automation and human creativity coexist harmoniously, supporting cognitive development and ultimately leading to a more enlightened society.

11

AI Learning Experiences for Cognitive Development

The Importance of Personalization in Learning

Personalization in learning is emerging as a cornerstone for enhancing cognitive development, especially in the age of artificial intelligence. Traditional educational models often adopt a one-size-fits-all approach, which can overlook the unique learning styles, paces, and preferences of individuals. By leveraging AI technologies, we can create tailored learning experiences that resonate with each learner's cognitive makeup. This personalized approach not only fosters engagement but also empowers learners to take ownership of their education, allowing them to navigate through complex information with greater ease and effectiveness.

AI-powered learning platforms are at the forefront of this personalization revolution. These platforms utilize data analytics and machine learning algorithms to assess individual performance, preferences, and areas of difficulty. By continually adapting to the learner's needs, these systems can present information in a way that aligns with their cognitive strengths and weaknesses. This targeted approach minimizes cognitive overload, ensuring that learners are neither overwhelmed by excessive information nor under-challenged by simplistic tasks. As a result, learners can achieve better retention of knowledge and enhance their critical thinking skills.

Moreover, personalized learning experiences can significantly reduce cognitive bias, which often hinders effective learning. AI systems can be designed to recognize and mitigate biased thinking patterns, presenting diverse perspectives and encouraging learners to approach problems from multiple angles. This not only cultivates a more nuanced understanding of complex subjects but also prepares learners to engage more thoughtfully in real-world scenarios. By equipping learners with the tools to recognize their biases, we foster an environment where critical thinking and open-mindedness thrive.

The design of AI interfaces plays a crucial role in facilitating mental clarity and focus. Intuitive, user-friendly designs can streamline cognitive processes, reducing distractions and enabling learners to concentrate on the task at hand. A well-designed AI interface not only enhances the learning experience but also promotes mindfulness, allowing learners to engage deeply with the material. This integration of mindfulness practices with AI tools can lead to improved attention spans and cognitive function, creating a harmonious balance between technology and human cognition.

Ultimately, the ethical use of AI in personalizing learning experiences is paramount. As we harness the power of AI to enhance cognitive skills, we must remain vigilant in ensuring that these technologies do not compromise our cognitive integrity. By prioritizing ethical considerations in the design and implementation of AI tools, we can create a future where technology not only supports but elevates our cognitive capabilities. Emphasizing personalization in learning represents a significant step toward achieving this goal, paving the way for a more informed, thoughtful, and creative society.

Techniques for Creating Personalized Experiences

Personalized experiences in AI applications can significantly enhance user engagement and cognitive development. One effective technique is adaptive learning algorithms, which tailor educational content based on individual user performance and preferences. By analyzing data on user interactions, these algorithms can identify strengths and weaknesses, allowing for a customized learning path that maximizes retention and understanding. This approach fosters an environment where users not only absorb information more effectively but also remain motivated to engage with the material, ultimately enhancing critical thinking skills.

Another technique involves the integration of user feedback loops within AI systems. By prompting users to reflect on their learning experiences and provide input on the content's relevance and difficulty, AI can continuously adjust to better meet their needs. This dynamic interaction not only helps in managing cognitive load by ensuring that users are neither overwhelmed nor under-challenged but also promotes a deeper connection with the material. Such feedback mechanisms can empower users, giving them a sense of ownership over their learning journey, which is critical for cognitive development.

Mindfulness practices can also be integrated into AI tools to enhance focus and reduce cognitive overload. AI can offer reminders and prompts for users to engage in mindfulness exercises, helping them to clear their minds before tackling complex tasks. This technique can be particularly beneficial in high-stress environments, where cognitive load may impede performance. By encouraging moments of reflection and mental clarity, AI applications can create a more conducive atmosphere for critical thinking and creativity, ultimately leading to improved outcomes in both personal and professional settings.

Designing interfaces that promote mental clarity is another crucial aspect of creating personalized experiences. User-friendly designs that prioritize simplicity and accessibility can significantly reduce cognitive strain. AI can analyze user behavior to optimize layout and functionality, ensuring that information is presented in a way that aligns with how users naturally process information. This not only enhances user satisfaction but also facilitates a more efficient cognitive workflow, allowing users to focus on decision-making and creative problem-solving rather than getting bogged down by complicated interfaces.

Finally, ethical considerations must guide the development of these personalized AI experiences. As AI systems become more adept at enhancing cognitive skills, it is vital to address potential biases that could affect learning outcomes. Employing strategies to mitigate cognitive bias—including ensuring diverse data sets and incorporating fairness algorithms—can help create equitable AI tools. By prioritizing ethical AI use, developers can ensure that personalized experiences foster genuine cognitive development while respecting and enhancing the unique capabilities of each individual user.

12

AI's Impact on Attention Span

Current Research Findings

Current research findings in the intersection of artificial intelligence and cognitive enhancement reveal a nuanced landscape where technology can significantly aid human cognition without compromising it. Recent studies indicate that AI tools, when designed thoughtfully, can enhance memory retention by providing personalized learning experiences tailored to individual cognitive profiles. Innovations such as adaptive learning platforms utilize algorithms to analyze a learner's progress and adapt content accordingly, effectively managing cognitive load. This tailored approach helps prevent overwhelm and encourages deeper engagement with the material, fostering improved retention and understanding.

Cognitive load management is a critical area of exploration in current research. AI applications that help filter information and present it in digestible formats allow users to focus on what truly matters. By utilizing machine learning algorithms to prioritize content based on relevance and user interaction, these tools effectively reduce extraneous cognitive stress. This is particularly beneficial in educational contexts where students often face an overload of information, enabling them to concentrate on essential concepts and critical thinking skills without distraction.

Furthermore, the integration of mindfulness practices within AI-powered learning platforms is gaining traction. Research suggests that incorporating mindfulness techniques can enhance focus and cognitive clarity, making learning experiences more effective. AI can facilitate these practices by offering reminders, personalized mindfulness exercises, and real-time feedback on attention levels.

Such integration not only supports mental well-being but also cultivates an environment conducive to deep learning and cognitive growth, enhancing the overall educational experience.

The design of AI interfaces plays a pivotal role in promoting mental clarity. Current findings indicate that user-friendly interfaces that minimize cognitive friction can lead to improved decision-making and creativity. By employing principles of human-centered design, researchers are developing AI systems that encourage users to engage more thoughtfully, rather than mindlessly interacting with technology. This emphasis on clear, intuitive design is crucial for balancing automation with human creativity, ensuring that AI serves as a supportive tool rather than a cognitive crutch.

Ethics in AI use is another area of significant research focus. As AI systems become more integrated into cognitive enhancement strategies, understanding the ethical implications is vital. Studies have shown that responsible AI design can aid in reducing cognitive biases by providing diverse perspectives and challenging established thought patterns. By prioritizing ethical considerations in the development of AI tools, researchers aim to create a landscape that not only enhances cognitive skills but also fosters critical thinking and equitable access to resources, ultimately benefiting society as a whole.

Future Directions in AI and Cognitive Research

As the landscape of artificial intelligence and cognitive research continues to evolve, it is crucial to explore innovative pathways that prioritize cognitive enhancement without compromising mental faculties. One promising direction is the development of AI tools specifically designed to improve memory retention. By leveraging machine learning algorithms that adapt to individual learning styles, these tools can provide personalized reinforcement techniques that enhance recall and retention. This customization not only addresses the unique cognitive profiles of users but also fosters a deeper understanding of the learning material, ultimately leading to more effective educational outcomes.

Cognitive load management is another vital area where AI can play a transformative role. AI applications can be engineered to assess and adapt the complexity of tasks in real time, ensuring that users are neither overwhelmed nor under-stimulated. By intelligently distributing cognitive demands, these systems can help maintain an optimal balance, allowing users to engage in complex problem-solving without experiencing mental fatigue. This approach not only enhances productivity but also preserves the user's cognitive resources for more creative and critical thinking tasks.

The integration of AI-powered learning platforms stands to revolutionize the way we foster critical thinking skills. Such platforms can employ advanced analytics to tailor educational content, encouraging learners to explore diverse perspectives and engage in reflective thinking. This not only enhances cognitive flexibility but also prepares users to navigate complex decision-making environments. By prioritizing critical thinking in educational contexts, we can cultivate a generation of learners who are better equipped to tackle the challenges of an increasingly complex world.

Mindfulness and AI integration represent an exciting frontier for improving focus and mental clarity. By utilizing AI to create personalized mindfulness routines that adapt to user behavior and preferences, we can enhance cognitive performance while promoting emotional well-being. These AI-driven mindfulness applications can help users develop greater self-awareness and concentration, ultimately leading to improved productivity and a more balanced mental state. This harmonious blend of technology and mindfulness can empower individuals to optimize their cognitive potential without sacrificing their mental health.

Finally, as we look toward the future, it is essential to prioritize ethical AI use in enhancing cognitive skills. This means designing AI interfaces that not only promote mental clarity but also encourage a balanced coexistence between automation and human creativity. Research should focus on developing AI strategies that actively reduce cognitive biases and foster personalized learning experiences. By understanding the nuanced impact of AI on attention spans and cognitive function, we can create systems that not only enhance cognitive capabilities but do so in a manner that respects and uplifts the human experience. Embracing this future will require collaboration among researchers, developers, and users to ensure that AI serves as a tool for empowerment rather than a source of cognitive compromise.

13

Future Trends in AI and Cognitive Enhancement

Emerging Technologies

Emerging technologies are reshaping the landscape of cognitive enhancement, presenting both opportunities and challenges for AI enthusiasts. As artificial intelligence continues to advance, it is crucial to explore how these technologies can be leveraged to enhance cognition without compromising our mental faculties. By focusing on applications that support memory retention, manage cognitive load, and promote critical thinking, we can create a future where AI acts as a partner in our cognitive development rather than a detractor.

AI-powered tools designed for memory enhancement are gaining traction, utilizing algorithms that adapt to individual learning styles and preferences. These platforms can provide personalized learning experiences, catering to each user's unique cognitive strengths and weaknesses. By integrating spaced repetition algorithms and adaptive learning techniques, these tools help users retain information more effectively, allowing them to build knowledge without overwhelming their cognitive capacities. This tailored approach not only fosters better memory retention but also encourages users to engage actively with the material, reinforcing their understanding and critical thinking skills.

Cognitive load management is another area where emerging technologies are making significant strides. With the increasing amount of information that individuals are exposed to daily, it is vital to develop AI applications that assist in filtering and organizing data. Intelligent systems can analyze user behavior and provide relevant content that aligns with their current focus, minimizing distractions and enabling deeper engagement. By designing interfaces that prioritize mental clarity and ease of use, developers can ensure that users remain focused on their tasks, ultimately enhancing their cognitive performance.

Mindfulness practices integrated with AI technologies are also emerging as powerful tools for improving focus and attention span. By leveraging AI to provide guided mindfulness exercises, users can cultivate a greater awareness of their thoughts and feelings, leading to improved cognitive function. These applications not only encourage users to take breaks and reflect but also help in reducing stress, which is often a significant barrier to effective cognitive performance. In this way, the integration of mindfulness and AI can create a balanced approach to cognitive enhancement, promoting mental well-being alongside productivity.

As we embrace these emerging technologies, it is essential to address the ethical implications of AI in cognitive enhancement. Striking a balance between automation and human creativity is vital to ensure that technology serves as a complement to our cognitive abilities rather than a crutch. Researchers and developers must prioritize ethical considerations in their designs, ensuring that AI tools empower users by reducing cognitive biases and fostering independent thinking. By cultivating a responsible approach to AI, we can harness the potential of these technologies to enhance cognitive skills while preserving the essence of human creativity and critical thinking.

Predictions for the Future of AI and Cognition

As we look toward the future of artificial intelligence and cognition, several exciting possibilities emerge that promise to enhance our cognitive capabilities while maintaining the integrity of our mental processes. The trajectory of AI development suggests a shift towards more personalized and adaptive learning experiences. AI systems will increasingly harness data to tailor educational content to individual learning styles and preferences, fostering environments where memory retention and critical thinking flourish. By focusing on the unique cognitive strengths and weaknesses of each user, AI can create a more engaging and effective learning experience, ultimately leading to deeper understanding and retention of knowledge.

In tandem with personalized learning, the design of AI interfaces will play a crucial role in promoting mental clarity and reducing cognitive load. Future AI tools will prioritize user experience by incorporating principles of cognitive psychology, ensuring that interactions are intuitive and seamless. This focus on user-centered design will enable individuals to engage with complex information without feeling overwhelmed. By minimizing distractions and streamlining workflows, these AI applications can enhance focus and productivity, allowing users to allocate their cognitive resources more effectively.

Moreover, the integration of mindfulness practices with AI technology holds significant potential for improving focus and attention span. As AI systems become more sophisticated, they will likely include features that encourage users to take regular breaks, practice mindfulness, and engage in reflective thinking. This integration can create a balanced approach to cognitive enhancement that not only leverages AI's strengths but also nurtures the human mind's inherent capabilities. Such synergies can lead to improved mental well-being and a more sustainable relationship with technology.

The ethical implications of using AI to enhance cognitive skills will continue to be a critical area of discussion. As AI tools become more prevalent in educational and workplace settings, it is essential to establish guidelines that promote responsible use. Ensuring that these technologies do not exacerbate cognitive biases or create disparities in access to cognitive enhancement will be paramount. As AI enthusiasts, we must advocate for transparent practices and the development of ethical frameworks that prioritize the well-being of users while maximizing cognitive potential.

Finally, the future of AI and cognition will likely see a growing emphasis on balancing automation with human creativity. While AI can handle repetitive tasks and analyze vast amounts of data more efficiently than humans, fostering an environment that encourages human creativity will be essential. By leveraging AI to augment human capabilities rather than replace them, we can create collaborative ecosystems where innovation thrives. This balance will not only enhance cognitive development but also ensure that the human touch remains integral to creative processes in an increasingly automated world.

14

Conclusion and Call to Action

Summary of Key Insights

The exploration of artificial intelligence and its intersection with human cognition reveals a tapestry of insights that can significantly enhance our understanding and application of AI technologies. Central to this discourse is the notion that AI can be harnessed to amplify cognitive capabilities without compromising the integrity of the mind. By leveraging AI tools designed to enhance memory retention, individuals can experience improved recall and information processing, allowing for a more efficient engagement with learning materials.

This suggests that when deployed thoughtfully, AI can serve as an ally in the quest for knowledge rather than a hindrance.

Cognitive load management is another critical area where AI can make a meaningful impact. As we navigate an increasingly information-rich environment, the ability to manage cognitive load becomes paramount. AI applications that intelligently curate content and streamline workflows enable users to focus on essential tasks, thereby reducing overwhelm and enhancing productivity. By integrating systems that prioritize user attention and filter distractions, AI can create an environment conducive to deep thinking and sustained engagement.

The integration of mindfulness practices with AI technologies presents a promising avenue for improving focus and cognitive clarity. AI-driven platforms can guide users in cultivating mindfulness through tailored exercises that promote mental well-being and attentiveness. This synergy not only fosters an environment where critical thinking thrives but also supports emotional resilience, ultimately enhancing overall cognitive performance. The potential for AI to facilitate mindfulness practices underscores the importance of designing tools that encourage a balanced approach to cognitive enhancement.

In the workplace, the delicate balance between automation and human creativity is crucial for fostering innovation. AI can augment human capabilities, allowing individuals to offload routine tasks while dedicating more time to creative problem-solving and strategic thinking. This collaborative model positions AI as a partner in the creative process, enabling teams to leverage their unique strengths while benefiting from the efficiencies provided by intelligent systems. As organizations embrace this partnership, the focus must remain on cultivating an environment that promotes both human ingenuity and technological advancement.

Finally, ethical considerations surrounding the use of AI in enhancing cognitive skills cannot be overlooked. As we advance in our understanding of AI's influence on attention span and cognitive function, it becomes imperative to develop strategies that mitigate cognitive bias and promote equitable access to personalized learning experiences.

Research in this domain highlights the potential for AI to tailor educational content to individual needs, fostering cognitive development in diverse populations. By prioritizing ethical practices in AI deployment, we can ensure that these technologies enrich our cognitive landscapes rather than detract from them.

Encouraging Responsible AI Engagement

Encouraging responsible engagement with AI is essential in ensuring that these powerful tools enhance our cognitive abilities rather than diminish them. As AI enthusiasts, we stand at a pivotal moment where the integration of AI into our daily lives can either support or hinder our mental processes. By prioritizing responsible AI use, we can create an environment that maximizes cognitive retention and minimizes distractions. This requires a collective effort to understand the balance between leveraging AI technologies and maintaining our cognitive integrity.

To foster responsible AI engagement, it is crucial to promote awareness of cognitive load management. AI tools have the potential to streamline tasks and enhance productivity, but they can also overwhelm users with excessive information and notifications. By designing AI applications that prioritize clarity and simplicity, we can help users focus on what truly matters, thereby optimizing their cognitive resources. This involves creating interfaces that encourage mindfulness, allowing users to engage with AI in a way that enhances their mental clarity rather than complicating it.

Moreover, the role of AI in education should emphasize critical thinking and creativity. AI-powered learning platforms can be tailored to deliver personalized experiences that cater to individual learning styles and preferences. By integrating adaptive learning techniques, these platforms can enhance memory retention and encourage deeper engagement with the material. However, educational AI must also challenge learners to think critically and creatively, rather than simply providing answers. This approach will help cultivate skills that are essential for navigating a complex world, ensuring that users are not just passive recipients of information.

Ethical considerations in the use of AI are paramount, especially when it comes to enhancing cognitive skills. The design of AI systems should inherently promote responsible use, avoiding reinforcement of cognitive biases. By employing strategies that actively work to reduce these biases, we can ensure that AI serves as a tool for enlightenment rather than a source of misinformation. This includes developing algorithms that prioritize diverse perspectives and challenge preconceived notions, fostering a more balanced approach to knowledge acquisition.

Finally, as we explore the intersection of mindfulness and AI, we must remain vigilant about the potential impact of these technologies on attention span and cognitive function. Mindful engagement with AI not only enhances focus but also encourages a deeper understanding of our cognitive processes. By creating AI systems that promote intentional use, we can support users in developing a more nuanced relationship with technology. This balance between automation and human creativity will empower individuals to harness AI's capabilities while preserving their cognitive health.

www.ingramcontent.com/pod-product-compliance
Lightning Source LLC
LaVergne TN
LVHW022012200926
848481LV00007B/2354
9798349312045